FOSTER

Design Monographs

FOSTER

ROBERT DIMERY

Norman Foster | London's skyline bristles with world-famous landmarks. The view from Waterloo Bridge takes in Sir Christopher Wren's seventeenth-century St Paul's Cathedral, the Victorian Palace of Westminster by Sir Charles Barry and Augustus Pugin, and twenty-first-century upstarts such as Renzo Piano's vertiginous Shard. Yet since Wren, no architect has transformed the face of the capital as thoroughly as Norman Foster.

Foster's curvaceous Swiss Re Building (now 30 St Mary Axe) ushered in a new era of super-tall high-rise buildings in the City of London, while his slimline Millennium Bridge offers a direct path between St Paul's and the art powerhouse of Tate Modern on the south bank of the River Thames. Further east stands his ovoid City Hall; further still, Canary Wharf's cavernous Tube station and the monolithic HSBC Tower. Stroll through the British Museum's light-filled Great Court, file into Wembley Stadium or the Royal Academy of Arts' Sackler Galleries, and you're on Foster territory.

Alongside inspired fellow travellers such as former business partner Richard Rogers, Foster broke with the historic conventions that had seen British architects' offices limited to a workforce of fewer than thirty staff, who generally produced conservative designs for exclusively UK-based projects. Commencing with his HSBC headquarters in Hong Kong (1985), he secured a string of ambitious and prestigious commissions, from the redevelopment of Berlin's Reichstag (1999) to France's awe-inspiring Millau Viaduct (2004) and Beijing's Capital International Airport (2008). Today, Foster + Partners is the UK's largest architecture firm, with offices worldwide and some 1,500 employees.

Like many of his illustrious peers (Rogers, Renzo Piano, Frank Gehry), Foster clearly has an appetite for such architectural exclamation marks, but has often emphasized the relevance of their urban context too. As a student, he studied civic spaces, including Siena's medieval Piazza del Campo, telling *ShortList* "This beautiful square [...] is one of the very first examples of a space that was actually planned. It serves as the spatial heart of the city."

Above. The Reichstag dome in Berlin, with its 360-degree view of the city, was constructed to direct sunlight into the building and to symbolize the reunification of Germany. The debating chamber of the Bundestag is visible directly below.

Above. Carré d'Art, Nîmes, 1993.

Foster created a broad new pedestrianized terrace for the front of the National Gallery in Trafalgar Square, replacing a busy road with a new common area. And while visiting the southern French city of Nîmes to make preparations for a new art museum, the Carré d'Art, he noticed that it lay on a popular route for pedestrians between the city's Roman amphitheatre and its largest park, the Jardins de la Fontaine. He designed the thoroughfare into his final scheme, creating a diagonal path through the building.

Foster's ambition to transcend the conventions of his industry has been a leitmotif of his career, whether that meant questioning a client's brief or pushing the limits of existing technology. It's a drive that he has honed since childhood.

Norman Robert Foster was born in 1935 and raised in working-class Levenshulme in Manchester. As a boy he became obsessed with machinery and mechanical movement, and would wait impatiently to get a glimpse of trains speeding by on the railway behind his house, while sketching the views from his bedroom window. Drawing remains a constant in his life: whether professionally or simply as a means of clarifying a point in conversation, he remains an inveterate doodler.

He adored the *Eagle*, a must-read comic for British schoolboys of the 1950s that featured Dan Dare – an unflappable space-age hero, though one clearly modelled on an RAF pilot. Created by Frank Hampson, the strip imagined a future of alluring, streamlined spacecraft and beguiling new worlds, all of which helped to stimulate Foster's lifelong passion for

The infrastructure that binds the architecture – by that I mean the squares, the parks, the connections – together is more important than the buildings themselves.
Norman Foster, *ShortList*, 2011

It never even occurred to me that there was a possibility of being an architect. I didn't know any architects. But I did read.
Norman Foster,
Financial Times, 2023

aeronautics. What's more, the *Eagle*'s centre pages featured detailed cutaway illustrations of engineering marvels, from racing cars and jets to Tube lines. "The future was always going to be better, was always brighter," he reminisced to the BBC's John Wilson in 2022. "Technology was the answer – and I still believe that, incidentally." Aged just seven, Foster produced his first design proper, for a single-seater aeroplane. Unsurprisingly, he also became a devotee of metal Meccano construction kits.

He'd also become fascinated with bicycles as a young teen (and remains so) – partly because of their mechanics, partly because of the freedom they offered. He rode off on long weekend jaunts with the Thame Valley Road Racing Cycle Club, to the Lake District, or to see the radio telescope at Macclesfield's Jodrell Bank observatory.

Levenshulme's library provided further inspiration. In his later teens, Foster would discover a brace of books there that introduced him to two masters of modernist architecture: Le Corbusier's *Towards a New Architecture* (first published in English in 1927) and *In the Nature of Materials* (1942), Henry-Russell Hitchcock's biography of Frank Lloyd Wright.

Although academically bright, Foster failed two of his nine O-Levels. Given their limited finances, his parents felt that he should start work and found him a place as a clerk in a treasurer's office at Manchester Town Hall, aged sixteen. The work proved uninspiring; the building itself, quite the reverse. "It's a masterpiece by a guy called Alfred Waterhouse, 1877," he enthused to the American Academy of Achievement in 2017. "And it's heroic. It's a noble building [...] You have light from above. You have the stained glass [...] You turn a corner, suddenly there's a soaring ceiling. It's about the spirits." Lunchtime walks provided more inspiration, not least when he chanced upon Sir Owen Williams' Art Deco *Daily Express* Building (1939) on Great Ancoats Street. Seemingly beamed down from a Dan Dare adventure, it boasted curved corners and expanses of glass curtain walling, alternating between opaque and black Vitrolite.

In 1953, he became an assistant at John E. Beardshaw and Partners, a local architecture practice. Three years later, he had enrolled at the University of Manchester's School of Architecture and City Planning, supplementing his studies with hours of research at Levenshulme's library, and – in 1959 – was formally recognized for his sharp-eyed draughtsmanship with a RIBA Silver Medal for a measured drawing of Bourn Windmill in Cambridgeshire. But things moved up a gear when he secured a postgraduate scholarship to study at Yale in 1961. (His Henry Fellowship also entitled him to a green card, meaning he could stay on and work in America afterwards.) Richard Rogers was a fellow student and the two swiftly bonded. In due course, they'd set off on extensive road trips with likeminded architectural aficionados, to see modernist masterpieces by the likes of Frank Lloyd Wright, and even visited the office of Mies van der Rohe.

One project in particular would have a long afterlife. Foster was tasked with designing a high-rise tower. Unconventionally, he asked to be allowed to collaborate with a structural engineer rather than work solo. "I felt empowered, as a designer, by knowing more about how that building would stand up," he recalled in 2022. "That knowledge helped shape the architecture of the building." The resulting design, in which elements such as the stairs, lifts and services were set to the side of the building rather than at its core, would be revived two decades later for his ground-breaking HSBC Headquarters in Hong Kong.

After graduating in 1962, Foster worked at architects on both the East and West coasts. But he was rapidly drawn back to the UK by a letter from Rogers with the offer of starting up a partnership. Named Team 4, the group united Rogers and his wife Su with Foster and his future wife – Wendy Cheesman. They were briefly joined by Wendy's sister Georgie, the only qualified architect among them.

Team 4 lasted only from 1963 to 1967, completing just two buildings. The first, Creek Vean (1965), is a flat-fronted, tall-windowed modernist Cornish riverside house, created for Marcus and Irene Brumwell, Su's parents. Its roofs and exterior steps were topped with grass (influenced by the terraced sod steps at Säynätsalo Town Hall in Finland, by Alvar Aalto), a feature that Foster revisited for his remarkable Willis Faber & Dumas Headquarters.

The second project, a multiple-use space designed in 1965 for electronics company Reliance Controls in Swindon, represented something more radical. Built in less than a year, the building's prefabricated parts made it highly cost-effective. Non-structural metal partitions inside could be repositioned, an example of "future-proofing" that later enabled a one-third increase in production area (and which would become a recurring feature of Foster's designs). Services were discreetly concealed: neon light tubes within the folds of the corrugated roof, hot and cold water within narrow pipes in the concrete flooring. It was also, in Foster's own words, a "democratic pavilion": in a challenge to contemporary working practices, both management and staff used the same entrance and shared all the facilities. Only a glass screen separated the factory from the company offices.

It was knocked down in 1991. Study surviving photographs today, and it may come across as rather an anonymous metal shed. But sixty years ago it was a revolutionary design – one informed by the team members' experiences Stateside, "Whether it was the Greyhound bus with the ribbed, polished stainless steel or [...] the Eames House, which was a catalogue assembly with expressed cross bracing," Foster reflected to *Dezeen* in 2019.

The scheme would influence several future Foster projects. For his Renault Distribution Centre (1981), also in Swindon, the architect again housed several facilities – car showroom, training area, workshops, offices, warehouse and restaurant – under one capacious roof, its PVC membrane dotted with skylights. The supporting cable-stayed masts and steel arches were bright yellow, a nod to the brand's livery.

The forward-thinking, egalitarian attitude that defined the design for Reliance Controls was to define Foster's approach to his first solo project, under the auspices of Foster Associates. That was the Fred Olsen Building

Opposite. Creek Vean, Cornwall, 1964. **Below.** Reliance Controls, Swindon, 1966, showing the corrugated steel and diagonal bracing.

(1969) in Millwall, for a shipping company in London's Docklands. Initially, the client simply envisaged a shed for the workforce with basic amenities, including showers. Foster – who heard about the job by chance – visited the site on spec, asked lots of questions and reworked the brief, creating something altogether bolder. The finished building was fronted by giant, bespoke glass sheets without any visible means of support, shipped from a company in Pittsburgh. It incorporated both dining and recreational zones

Above. The fully glass northern wall of Reliance Controls, Swindon, 1966.

and – as at Reliance Controls – management and workers shared them.
Artwork from the owner's private collection adorned the walls upstairs.

The success of the design attracted IBM, who commissioned Foster
to create a temporary head office in Cosham. It's still standing today, and
Grade- II listed. Why? Rather than the short-life huts that IBM proposed,
Foster delivered an eye-catching block faced with bronze glass, reflecting
and visually blending with its wooded surroundings.

Illuminated with ample natural light, it could accommodate up to 1,000 workers and incorporated multiple facilities, meaning that IBM didn't need any more buildings on the site. As with Reliance Controls, services were tucked away – electrical wiring ran through hollow metal columns – and the space could be reconfigured. All within eighteen months, and under budget. Such pioneering designs attracted multiple awards, and proved that businesses could have faith in Foster Associates. Their next project would impress even more.

It's still a surprise to come across the graceful, bronze-tinted glass walls of the Willis Faber & Dumas head office (1975; today the Willis Building) in Ipswich. Suspended from a perimeter cantilever, they were inspired by memories of Manchester's *Daily Express* Building – although Mies van der Rohe envisaged something similar in 1919 for a never-built Berlin high-rise. The manufacturer, Pilkington, had provided the glazed exterior for the IBM head office, but had never produced anything taller than one storey so far. Foster pushed them and the result was an arresting three-floor curtain wall. (He would later collaborate with Pilkington at the Reichstag in Berlin.) Set in a piano-like profile dictated by Ipswich's medieval street layout, its curves reflect the nearby cityscape and, along with its low profile, help the structure to blend in.

The building bucked convention in other ways too, from the liberal areas of greenery and spacious, triple-height foyer, to its open-plan offices, indoor swimming pool and gym for employees and turfed rooftop garden – which also provided insulation. (The citation for Foster's 1999 Pritzker Prize noted, tellingly: "In the early seventies, he pioneered the notion that the workplace could be a pleasant environment.") It's also proof positive of Foster's maxim that "As an architect you design for the present, with an awareness of the past, for a future that is essentially unknown." The building incorporated raised office floors; when computers became an office commonplace, it was already set up to allow for their wiring.

When you drive up to the IBM building it isn't there.
A+U Magazine, 1971

Previous page. IBM Pilot Head Office, Cosham, 1971. **Above.** The design for the Climatroffice by Norman Foster and Buckminster Fuller, 1971.

Foster's "Green Agenda for Architecture" (the title of a lecture he gave in 2017) was greatly inspired by his friendship with inventor and philosopher R. Buckminster Fuller. Deviser of the geodesic dome, Fuller was a committed environmentalist whose *Operating Manual for Spaceship Earth* (1969) explored the choices facing humanity given the limited and dwindling resources of our planet. He also questioned architectural assumptions, proposing lighter, more energy-efficient structures.

In 1971, Foster and Buckminster Fuller devised a bold new model for workplaces, one that would directly influence the scheme for the Willis Faber & Dumas Headquarters. The Climatroffice would create adaptable, multi-level workspaces incorporating shared gardens, within its own microclimate, all under a diagonal grid (or diagrid) structure. The diagrid consciously harked back to the inspired designs of Russian engineer Vladimir Shukhov. His startling works included Moscow's Shabolovka Radio Tower (1922), whose light, diagrid latticework and hyperboloid curves provided great structural strength, enabling it to rise to 160 metres (525 feet).

Triangular forms offered well-established architectural advantages: with sturdy joints, any side of a structural triangle can withstand pressure as it is supported by the two remaining sides. "Nature's own system of coordination [is] based on triangles," observed Fuller, who incorporated the shape into his own geodesic domes and whose designs did much to popularize them in the later twentieth century.

Steel diagrid structures would grace the outer skins of several iconic Foster constructions, notably the dome of the British Museum's Great Court, London's 30 St Mary Axe (also known as the Gherkin) and the Hearst Tower in New York. "A series of triangles that combine gravity and lateral support into one, making the building stiff, efficient, and lighter than a traditional high-rise," as Yoram Eilon, the Hearst Tower's project manager, put it. Many other architects have employed the same design – see Zaha Hadid's Zaragoza Bridge Pavilion in Spain, or Herzog & de Meuron's Prada store in Tokyo – but the diagrid surely owes its popularization to Foster.

Fuller's interest in streamlining construction materials, and the use of tensile structures, fed into a particular strand of modernist architecture, largely British in origin, expressed in the work of (among others) Foster, Richard Rogers, Michael and Patricia Hopkins, Nicholas Grimshaw and Renzo Piano: "high-tech". Broadly, the term encompasses the use of techniques and materials associated with industrial design, such as readily interchangeable, prefabricated components – often made from steel, aluminium or glass – open-plan, adaptable spaces, expansive roofs and proudly exposed working parts. Of this last, the most famous examples are Piano and Rogers' Pompidou Centre in Paris (1977) and Richard Rogers Partnership's Lloyd's Building in London (1986), both textbook "inside-

It was truly the first breathing, naturally ventilated building with filtered air.
Norman Foster, *Dezeen*, 2020

out" designs. These proved hugely controversial and seemed strikingly futuristic, although at least one key influence was Victorian: Joseph Paxton's 1851 modular cast iron and plate glass Crystal Palace exhibition hall. "That really was the birth of modern architecture, of prefabrication, of soaring spans of transparency," Foster told *Dezeen* in 2019. "That is truly high-tech."

His reputation burnished by the Willis Faber & Dumas head office, Foster found himself in line to design a unique structure in the grounds of the University of East Anglia campus in Norwich. Sir Robert and Lady Sainsbury wanted a bespoke venue for their valuable art collection, which they were donating to the university. Foster's proposal was for a hangar-like facility devoid of internal supporting columns. Its latticed, tubular steel frame wrapped in an aluminium skin (later replaced with white steel, owing to an unforeseen rust incursion) would arch over a vast open central space that served as exhibition area, teaching space and restaurant, each divided by moveable partitions. It was another in a long line of Foster's challenges to a brief: the Sainsburys had originally imagined discreet buildings for separate facilities.

Light enters through enormous glass walls front and back and filters through louvres in the partly glazed rooftop, allowing views down to a lake and across verdant expanses to the university proper. In a last-minute flash of inspiration, Foster decided that auxiliary rooms, services and all the prosaic elements that the building required to function, should be housed within a gap 2.4 metres (8 feet) wide within the steel trusswork, leaving the floor uncluttered. Although this double membrane had the added benefit of facilitating insulation within the structure, the late change, and other unforeseen structural corrections, pushed the project seriously over budget. But the Sainsburys were delighted. At an awards ceremony twenty years later, Sir Robert praised the building as his most prized work of art.

The Sainsbury Centre was Foster's first public building, and led indirectly to him tendering a bid for what would become his first major international commission. This new project would change the whole nature of Foster Associates, enabling it to expand and assume a global presence, while also helping to stave off bankruptcy at a time when many peers were going bust.

Opposite. Sainsbury Centre, Norwich, 1978.

The commission came with weighty political overtones. Anticipating the transfer of Hong Kong back to China in 1997, bankers HSBC wanted to create a new statement building to replace its old headquarters, signalling continuity and confidence that the face of capitalism would be unchanged by the handover.

The brief suggested the options of demolishing the existing structure entirely (while ensuring that banking operations continued uninterrupted), or keeping its banking hall and erecting a tower alongside. As was his wont, Foster went the extra mile, quizzing HSBC's staff forensically about how they operated and even – respectful of Chinese traditions – commissioning a feng shui geomancer. Equally characteristically, he reworked the bank's brief for them, suggesting a "phased regeneration" in stages, which would allow HSBC to have ongoing input even as construction was underway.

Approved in 1981, Foster's final proposal audaciously redefined the concept of the skyscraper. The building comprises three bays, bookended by eight paired masts – each comprising four steel columns linked together – that support the full weight of the superstructure. It has a stepped profile of three towers, the tallest forty-four floors high, running east to west. Vertically, the building is divided into five zones (dubbed "villages"), with the masts supporting five double-height suspension trusses. Each floor is suspended from a truss via tubular steel hangers; the floors vary in depth and width as they rise up the building. Two-storey-deep X-shaped braces, which span between the trusses, offer stability along the bank's north–south axis. The structure allowed for simultaneous downward and upward construction.

That was just as well: Foster Associates had just four years to complete it. As time was limited, and Hong Kong then lacked the necessary industry expertise, Foster again opted for precision-engineered prefabricated components, to be shipped from Europe, Japan and the USA. Mirrors set on a mobile "sunscoop" directed light down through the yawning atrium to the ground-floor plaza, helping to conserve energy, while the air-conditioning system utilized seawater drawn up through a broad tunnel dug through the rock below. To free up the atrium, all central services, stairs and lifts were placed on the side of the building, an innovation that harked back to one of Foster's Yale-era exercises.

The scheme had flexibility hardwired into it, allowing for later changes to office spaces that would include – though Foster's team could not have

Above. A drawing of the HSBC Headquarters, Hong Kong, 1986.

anticipated it – the incorporation of a dealers' room. A future that is essentially unknown indeed. Or, as both Foster and Richard Rogers put it in interviews, "The only constant is change."

The project went massively over budget, costing some $688 million (around £1.8 billion today) and became widely regarded as history's most expensive building. But it triumphantly delivered on HSBC's daunting brief to have the best bank headquarters in the world. Foster's visionary creation "tore up the rule book and influenced how commercial blocks and entire financial centres have been made ever since", marvelled *The Guardian* thirty years later. Not bad for your first project above three storeys. Foster would later build HSBC's London headquarters, Eight Canada Square (2002), and the nearby Canary Wharf Tube station (1999) – all smooth grey concrete walls and cathedral-like spaces. (The station took inspiration from his scheme for Bilbao's metro, famed for its shell-like "Fosterito" entrance awnings.)

Since the 1980s, Foster's studio has been developing industrial design products alongside all that game-changing architecture. In 1981, his studio developed its own adjustable table for use in the office, variants of which were subsequently used in the Renault Distribution Centre. A commission from Italy's Tecno saw this develop into the ergonomically friendly Nomos table and desking system (both 1987). Naturally enough, since then his office has devised plenty more sleek, award-winning products for work and home, among them the Foster 550 lamp, an elegant luminaire for Louis Poulsen (2007), and the software-generated curves of the Arc table for Molteni (2009). Unsurprisingly, he has also turned his attention to aircraft, notably the Dassault Falcon 7X (2009) business jet for NetJets. And as with Foster + Partners' (the name of his practice since 1999) construction projects, architects and engineers collaborated to create the svelte and speedy Izanami motor yacht for Lürssen (1995).

The late 1980s were a challenging time for Norman Foster. His beloved wife and business partner Wendy died from cancer in 1989 aged just fifty-one, leaving him to care for their four sons, two of whom were adopted. A second marriage, to jewellery designer Sabiha Rumani Malik, lasted just four years, but his third – to Elena Ochoa, a publisher and art curator – has proved happier; they have two children.

Foster Associates kicked off the 1990s by setting up a new riverside studio in Battersea, an open-plan, double-height space that remains the firm's London office. They had their first triumph of the decade with the Torre de Collserola (1992), a communications/broadcasting tower in the hills above Barcelona, whose innovative concrete- and steel-braced column is a mere 4.5 metres

Below. Nomos desk for Tecno, 1987.

(14¾ feet) across at its base, and which was designed to accommodate future technologies. Catalonia's primary telecommunications hub, it was built ahead of the Olympic Games held in Barcelona in 1992, but remains much loved by sightseers for the panoramic views from the platform on its tenth floor.

Foster Associates' redevelopment of the Sackler Galleries in the Royal Academy of Arts (1991) replaced the unloved Diploma Galleries on the top floor. The practice's solution offered access both from the Palladian main Academy building and from a Victorian block at the rear. In the narrow courtyard between them, Foster inserted an elegant glass-sided lift and staircase. A reception area outside the Sackler rooms, which are top lit with both artificial and natural light, incorporates glazed floor panels along the side, spilling light into the courtyard below, while sculptures are displayed on a parapet of the Victorian block.

As a modern-day intervention sensitive to historic architecture, it succeeded admirably. Ditto the Carré d'Art (1993). This combined museum of contemporary art and library in Nîmes, southern France, faces the Maison Carrée, a superbly preserved first-century Roman temple. Its concrete, steel and glass structure might have created a clash between the two in other hands, but instead Foster's design sets up a dialogue – as reflected in the deep, columned portico whose proportions echo those of its ancient neighbour. The Carré d'Art stands nine storeys high, but five of them are set below ground, aligning its profile with neighbouring buildings. And the light-filled central atrium alludes to the inner courtyards common to the region.

Foster was also to produce two innovative new structures for Germany. The first, Frankfurt's Commerzbank (1997), is Germany's tallest building at 259 metres (850 feet). Cited by Foster + Partners as "the world's first ecological office tower", this triangular building's fifty-six floors incorporate a two-layer skin, which allows for natural ventilation as well as helping to conserve energy: air enters via slots in the outer façade. The system is complemented by nine hanging "sky gardens", each some 15 metres (49 feet) high, arranged in a spiral up the vertical extent of the building, which the bank's website describes as its "green lungs". As with earlier projects, Foster's design set the supply conduits at the tower's corners, allowing natural light to fill its core.

The second project was on another scale altogether. With the reunification of Germany at the start of the 1990s, the national parliament would move from

Bonn to Berlin. The Reichstag – the site of a fire in 1933, bombed in the Second World War and then subject to questionable rebuilding – was to be its new home, but would require a major overhaul to signal the new era. There was a raft of obstacles to navigate, not all of them architectural. Right-wing politicians wanted to restore the original iron and glass dome destroyed in the war. There were arguments over the seating arrangement and debates about the design of the heraldic eagle in the new parliamentary chamber. What's more, parliamentarians regularly contacted the press after ostensibly private meetings with Foster, resulting in an almost live running commentary in the media.

Foster worked through twenty-six alternative schemes before one was accepted. In his final design, a cupola was installed on the rooftop, accessible via two spiral ramps within, offering the public the chance to enjoy breathtaking views, not only outwards across the German capital but also inwards, down to the debating chamber of the national parliament, the Bundestag, via a glass ceiling. According to Foster, this is a literal embodiment of transparent government, as the politicians are constantly under public scrutiny – although, as critics pointed out, how does that work if you can't hear them?

Mirrors lining a tapering central cone within the dome reflected daylight down into the building, reducing the need for artificial light, while a sun shield traces the sun's path, blocking its glare and reducing excess heat. The "sunscoop" at the HSBC Headquarters was an influence here, although in *Makers of Modern Architecture* (2007), Martin Filler cites similar light columns in the entrance hall of Berlin's Grosses Schauspielhaus theatre (1919) by Hans Poelzig.

The air-conditioning is powered by biofuel, in the form of refined vegetable oil, which reduces CO_2 emissions by around 90 per cent. A deep underground aquifer serves as a store for surplus heat, which can be pumped up to warm the building. So modest are the Reichstag's energy needs that it reportedly consumes less energy than it generates.

Foster replaced the original neo-Baroque interior with a voluminous open space. But behind glass panelling, he preserved graffiti left by Russian troops when they stormed the building, an event captured in Yevgeny Khaldei's iconic image *Raising a Flag Over the Reichstag* (1945).

Opposite. Sackler Galleries, London, 1991.

Foster's first major work of the decade had been a second terminal building at London Stansted Airport, an achievement that would have far-reaching consequences in terms of the practice's reputation and future projects.

Given his lifelong enthusiasm for flight (he's an experienced pilot and has flown gliders, jets and helicopters), it's little wonder that Foster disliked traditional airports, with their confused layouts, weighty roofs blocking out daylight, and restricted views. Instead, he went back to basics, seeking inspiration from the design of the oldest airports.

Stansted's design optimized natural light and clear sight lines for travellers: surrounded by four glass walls, in a single vast space, they could easily orient themselves, even without signs. Above is a lightweight, lattice-domed roof supported by steel "trees"; to make this possible, air-conditioning and electrical services – hitherto housed on top, requiring a heavy, solid roof to support them – were laid underground, filtering up to the concourse within ducts in their trunks, rather than cluttering up roof space.

It was nice while it lasted. Predictably, the terminal was soon full of retail kiosks and outlets, while exponentially increasing passenger numbers required further redevelopment. Nevertheless, Foster's considered approach helped revolutionize modern airport design and served as a template for the hugely ambitious Chek Lap Kok airport (1998) for Hong Kong. Again, the plan

An airport should be a celebratory structure. It should combine a strong visual identity with a humanistic sense of clarity so that the experience of air travel is uplifting, secure, welcoming and efficient.
Norman Foster, *Icon*, 2021

Above. Terminal at Stansted Airport, London, 1991.

created an unobstructed, easily navigable space, aided by overhead skylights pointing in a single direction. It housed a lightweight, vaulted roof devoid of bulky service equipment, though here gently undulating as opposed to Stansted's straight edges; appropriately enough, from above the 1.2-kilometre (¾-mile) structure resembles the outline of an aircraft. To create the space for it, land had to be reclaimed to quadruple the area of Chek Lap Kok island, and a 100-metre (328-foot) peak reduced to just 7 metres (23 feet).

On completion it was the world's largest airport terminal, before being superseded by another Foster project – Terminal 3 of Beijing Capital International Airport (2008). This had to be completed in a mere four years in order to be ready for that year's Olympic Games in Beijing, and at one stage involved around 50,000 workers. The world's largest airport terminal on completion, at some 1.3 million square metres (14 million square feet), it was designed to accommodate 50 million people per year by 2020. Foster's design shows sensitivity to regional traditions in its graceful, dragon-like form and colour scheme, which changes from rich imperial reds to golden yellows as passengers travel through the site.

Topped with a capacious aerodynamic, latticed roof, Beijing Capital is intended to minimize passengers' journey and transfer times within the building, and keep floor-level changes to a minimum. The skylights line up with the south-east, to ensure maximum heat gain from the sun on winter mornings, reducing energy consumption, while shading was incorporated into the design to help keep the building cool. In a phrase that could be applied to any number of his buildings, Foster once described Beijing's airport as a "celebration of space and light".

The new millennium had opened with two landmark commissions for London – and generated rare criticism for Foster. The Millennium Bridge (2000) was the first new crossing between the north and south banks of the Thames for a century, lined up perfectly between St Paul's Cathedral and Tate Modern (on the site of the former Bankside Power Station, designed by Sir Giles Gilbert Scott). Silver and slimline, discreetly low-lying, it seemed an understated and highly effective design.

Opposite. Millennium Bridge, London, 2000.

The project united Foster + Partners with sculptor Sir Anthony Caro and Arup, the celebrated engineering firm whose CV includes the rebuilding of Coventry Cathedral, the Sydney Opera House, the Pompidou Centre and Barcelona's Sagrada Familia. Quite the triumvirate. All the more embarrassing, therefore, that the bridge began to swing alarmingly under the feet of its first users, whose natural tendency to try and stabilize themselves by pushing their weight against the sway only exacerbated it. Two days after it opened it had to close – for two years. The celebratory Millennium Bridge became the "Wobbly Bridge".

None of Arup's preparatory tests had flagged up anything remotely like this. Shouldn't the bridge's eight supporting suspension cables, pulling with a combined weight of 2,000 tonnes, have been more than enough to keep it stable? As it turned out, the problem (formally, "synchronous lateral excitation") wasn't unique to this structure. Any footbridge over a certain length, with a certain number of people walking over it, would be vulnerable to the same effect – and around 90,000 pedestrians made the crossing on the bridge's opening weekend. There was a famous precedent a little further west along the Thames. Alarming vibrations caused by traffic had once seen the Albert Bridge unflatteringly dubbed the "Trembling Lady". It still features notices that warn troops to break step as they cross.

Arup's solution was to add X-shaped braces and a plenitude of dampers to absorb the shocks from footsteps, all integrated neatly within the structure. Since reopening in February 2002, the Millennium Bridge has remained reassuringly still – but the experience tainted Foster and his practice, by association.

On 6 December 2000, the late Queen Elizabeth II opened Foster's new Great Court at the heart of the British Museum. A latticed steel and glass dome, partly influenced by that of the Reichstag, floated majestically above an open 0.8-hectare (2-acre) space that housed the famous Reading Room. Foster had referred back to the building's original design by Robert Smirke, which had envisaged a central courtyard garden, but from the 1850s onwards the British Library's paraphernalia gradually encroached on the space. The opportunity to reclaim it as a public area, and much-needed thoroughfare between rooms, only came in 1997, when the library moved across town to St Pancras.

Foster's scheme created Europe's largest covered square, under a digitally modelled roof comprising more than 3,212 unique glass panes. It's fixed to the court's perimeter walls on sliding bearings, allowing it to move and adapt to temperature changes. The court itself is lined with Balzac limestone. The museum's overall space increased by 40 per cent with its integration, and two additional galleries were also added.

So far, so splendid. But English Heritage swiftly raised protests over the choice of the "inferior" French limestone – Anstrude Roche Claire – for the court's south portico, which has an altogether lighter complexion than that of the rest of the building. A museum official insisted they'd been assured that Portland stone would be used, in keeping with Smirke's original plans. True, the contract was vaguely worded, stating only that the material should be "an oolitic limestone (Portland limestone from the Base Bed or similar)". And ultimately it was the stone's supplier, rather than Foster + Partners, that was responsible. But the design itself drew flak too. While praising the dome in *Prospect*, Rowan Moore bemoaned the courtyard and its "beige, respectable stone arranged with deadening symmetry. A pompous double stair rises to almost nowhere amid a shapeless plenitude of space. Stone is cut and polished with such precision as to look like plastic."

Foster's next major project was again in London, this time within the square mile of the City. The Swiss Re Building (2003; now 30 St Mary Axe) is still best known as the Gherkin, owing to the way its modest footprint swells around the midriff, then tapers towards the nose cone. Owned by Swiss Re, a reinsurance company (i.e. insurers of insurers), it became the first City building in twenty-five years to break the 180-metre (590-foot) bar – leading the dean of St Paul's to fret that it would vie with his cathedral's dome. The Gherkin was to usher in a new era of high-rise towers for Central London, driven partly by a corporate appetite for ever-larger structures (it has 50,000 square metres/54,000 square feet of office space) to allow for buyouts and mergers. But its distinctive form also owes something to Foster's belief that vertical density and a smaller footprint make for a more sustainable design.

Built on the site of the Baltic Exchange, which was destroyed by an IRA bomb in 1992, the forty-one-storey edifice is certainly ambitious. Unlike rectilinear skyscrapers, its distinctive shape encourages winds to flow smoothly across its surface, easing turbulence for pedestrians below and reducing heat loss across its face. It also allows for more public space in the plaza below.

Inside, an open atrium spirals upwards. Each floor is rotated five degrees from those below and above, with light wells serving clusters of six floors, and it incorporates air shafts that – in tandem with the offset design – were intended to produce natural ventilation for around 40 per cent of the year. The Gherkin is sheathed in a double skin: the outer layer a double-glazed diagrid, incorporating flaps to allow rising hot air to escape; the inner counterpart comprising sliding glass doors.

Widely lauded on its completion, 30 St Mary Axe secured the 2004 Stirling Prize, while a poll of top architects' firms hailed it as "the most admired new building in the world". Foster + Partners proudly dubs it "London's first ecological tall building". Less happily, although Swiss Re occupied some of the lower floors, the building initially struggled to attract other tenants – possibly because it remained so closely identified with Swiss Re. Faults with the windows caused problems with the natural ventilation system, meaning that mechanical ventilation had to be used instead. Many tenants walled off access to the atrium. And, particularly before a crop of other high-rise towers began sprouting here, it certainly disrupted the skyline.

For some onlookers, the entire episode was another example of the rampant egoism of contemporary starchitects such as Foster. "What's it for?" asked London Design Museum co-founder Stephen Bayley in *The Independent* in October 2002, of the still-incomplete building. "And who really benefits from parking this 600-foot ego-trip in the middle of our capital city?"

The erection of 30 St Mary Axe heralded a boom time for spectacular architecture in and around the City of London, with statement buildings such as 122 Leadenhall Street (the Cheese Grater), 20 Fenchurch Street (the Walkie-Talkie) and the Shard – London's sentinel (or Dark Tower of Mordor?) all competing for attention. Similarly, while the revamped Battersea Power Station is a majestic and engaging building – albeit one packed to the rafters with high-end retail – are the clusters of surrounding luxury apartment blocks an eye-dazzling showcase for name architects (Frank Gehry and Foster included), or simply a dizzying clash? In a 2017 interview for the *Evening Standard*, Stephen Bayley complained, "Buildings need to work in context. Developers are

Above. The Gherkin (30 St Mary Axe), London, 2003.

It's not enough to come up with a beautiful object – you've got to deal with the reality of what's going to go on inside. His buildings are actually complete without the people.
Carolyn Steel, architect, *The Guardian*, 2002

greedy, local authorities are often stupid, and most architects wanton and obsequious." And the Shard? "A big bloody middle finger to London".

Hackles were raised over another Foster scheme, to be located not far from 30 St Mary Axe. Nicknamed the Tulip, 20 Bury Street would have risen 305 metres (1,000 feet) into the air but was dismissed outright in November 2021 by the UK government, with housing secretary Michael Gove citing problems of embodied carbon costs and the building's likely impact on views of the nearby Tower of London.

The Tulip proved to be one phallic protuberance too many, but Foster has long championed the concept of high-density, high-rise buildings as a more sustainable option. His Millennium Tower for London (eventually superseded by 30 St Mary Axe) would have stretched 386 metres (1,266 feet) into the air – not far off Vladimir Tatlin's extraordinary, never-built Constructivist tower from the early twentieth century. Meanwhile, the 180-floor, cone-shaped Tokyo Millennium Tower would have topped out at a giddy 840 metres (2,755 feet). For many, this smacked of the kind of hubris that turns cities into battlegrounds for architectural one-upmanship. Neither project went ahead.

Happily, and despite initial reservations from locals, the Sage Gateshead (2004) cultural centre on the banks of the River Tyne has proved a resounding success. Its undulating glass and steel roof shelters three standalone auditoria – two for concerts and one for a music school. The concrete used for its construction incorporates more air bubbles than usual, to produce optimum acoustics and soundproofing. The main 1,700-seater hall is covered in a range of woods to improve its resonance, while six wooden baffle panels hanging over the stage, and sound-absorbent curtains, offer further acoustic refinement – a must when your venue is home to an acclaimed chamber orchestra such as the Royal Northern Sinfonia.

Foster returned to the diagrid for another unconventional design, this time in New York. His Hearst Tower (2006) rises from a six-storey Art Deco building created by Joseph Urban for the media magnate William Randolph Hearst in 1928. Urban's boxy structure now serves as a plinth for Foster's forty-four-storey edifice, whose eye-catching zig-zag silhouette results from corners cutting between diagonals. Its sustainability credentials sound impressive too: the diamond grid lattice employs 20 per cent less steel than a traditional design would, while overall the structure incorporates 85 per cent recycled steel. Moreover, for nine months of the year, the tower's ventilation and cooling employs outside air. The US Green Building Council's Leadership in Energy and Environmental Design programme awarded it Manhattan's first gold rating.

The New Yorker's Paul Goldberger was bowled over, famously dubbing Foster the "Mozart of Modernism" and praising the building for "energizing" the city's skyline; likewise *The New York Times*, whose Nicolai Ouroussoff felt that the Hearst Tower "may be the most muscular symbol of corporate self-confidence to rise in New York since the 1960s, when Modernism was in full bloom, and most Americans embraced technological daring as a sure route to social progress". Look back at Hong Kong's HSBC Headquarters and you'll find a bank eager to project that same soaring "corporate self-confidence", and doing so via high-tech.

Not everyone was convinced. In 2008, Robert Campbell speculated in the *Architectural Record* that (heresy!) much of the impressive trusswork was structurally unnecessary. He also despaired at the tower's lack of engagement with Urban's original structure: "Works of architecture, whatever they do, should not express contempt for the other buildings they must live among." For Campbell, violent disparity between styles is not of itself a virtue.

Rowan Moore is a kindred spirit: in *Slow Burn City* (2016), he argues that extreme contrast "undervalues the uses of rapport, affinity and the ability to operate in different registers, to be both alike and different at once".

Around the start of the new millennium, Foster + Partners began to utilize computer-aided design. Its scheme for Stansted Airport benefited from it, as did the Chesa Futura (2004) in St Moritz. The latter's rounded form –

Above. Chesa Futura, St Moritz, 2004.

unusual for an architect whose previous buildings had mostly been rectilinear – were partly made possible by this new technology, which allowed components to be modelled on screen, and cut precisely in a factory, again via computer. These were then finished with a covering of a quarter of a million larch shingles – locally sourced and cut by a septuagenarian craftsman.

As other leading architects were also discovering (Frank Gehry and Zaha Hadid spring to mind), digitally driven design and manufacture allowed both for incredible precision and the ability to create buildings with more complex geometries. Another Foster project, the YachtPlus vessel (2005), would have been hugely time-consuming had it been purely hand-modelled; 3D printing allowed for unprecedented accuracy and the ability to adapt a design quickly and efficiently.

Foster + Partners' majestic design for the Millau Viaduct (2004) above the Tarn Valley in southern France – a collaboration with structural engineer Michel Virlogeux – ranks among the greatest triumphs within its portfolio. At 343 metres (1,125 feet), it is the world's tallest bridge. It takes just a minute to cross its 2,460-metre (8,069-foot) span, and since opening it has both reduced heavy traffic near the town of Millau and helped reduce travel times to the Mediterranean. Its elegant expanse is supported by 154 steel stays that radiate from seven monumental concrete pillars. In 2015, Foster rhapsodized about its environmental benefits to *The Observer*'s Rowan Moore: "Millau cut out five-hour traffic jams, which mean that the saving in CO_2 from the 10 per cent traffic that is heavy goods vehicles had an effect equivalent to a forest of 40,000 trees."

Above. Spaceport America, New Mexico, 2014.

His ability to produce surprising work that doesn't feel labored must drive his competitors crazy.
Paul Goldberger,
The New Yorker, 2005

Ten years after the Millau Viaduct, his practice produced Spaceport America, a commercial space terminal sunk into the New Mexico desert whose rusty hued, low-lying roof – reminiscent of a manta ray from above – blends smoothly with the surrounding landscape and takes advantage of westerly winds to provide natural ventilation. Its passive cooling and heating systems incorporate underground "earth tubes": air drawn through them is preheated in winter and precooled in summer, substantially reducing energy consumption.

Through high glass windows, visitors can watch spacecraft depart and land on the runway outside. As with Stansted, as with Beijing, Spaceport America is designed to convey the thrill of lifting off into the blue beyond, something that has never left their creator.

Architecture and aeronautics dovetail neatly for this architect, who once compared the technology of an aircraft's cantilevered wing with that which enables the balconies at Fallingwater (1939), Frank Lloyd Wright's house in Pennsylvania's Laurel Highlands, to stretch out expansively over the waterfall below. So naturally, Foster was honoured when asked to design the American Air Museum in Duxford, Cambridgeshire (1997). Such a commission was almost inevitable: after all, several of his works have been inspired by the shape of an aircraft hangar (notably the Sainsbury Centre). He won a Stirling Prize for the museum's discreet, graceful design: a shell-like concrete roof that arcs over a host of historic US warplanes – some suspended from the ceiling – and descends into a grassy bank to the rear. To the front, a vast window looks out over the runway.

Of Foster's more recent completed projects, perhaps the most talked-about is Apple Park (2018), a corporate campus centred on a giant circular "groundscraper" in Cupertino, California. Plans that began with Apple co-founder Steve Jobs himself resulted in a 260,000-square metre (2.8-million square foot) corporate headquarters – The Ring. Covering 71 hectares (175 acres), this huge circle is flanked inside and out by some 9,000 drought-resistant trees and indigenous plants. Its outside is covered in 800 curved glass panels, each 13.7 metres (45 feet) tall. Another nickname is The Spaceship, and indeed it's not hard to imagine the gleaming edifice one day rising silently to the stars. Its street address, after all, is 1 Infinite Loop. Par for the course with a Foster + Partners project, it employs natural ventilation, reportedly functions without artificial heating or cooling for nine months of the year and is touted as one of the most sustainable buildings on the planet, with solar panels that generate 17 megawatts of power. Its runs on 100 per cent renewable energy.

Many of Foster's buildings aspire to inspire, in a way comparable to the effect that medieval cathedrals had on congregations – something very much in Steve Jobs' mind when he was planning Apple Park. Think big, think innovatory, and hang the cost per square metre. "I think we have a shot at building the best office building in the world," he claimed in 2011.

On the downside, some employees apparently walked straight into those expansive glass walls without seeing them. Some critics argued that the campus exacerbated urban sprawl and monopolized a vast area that could have been dedicated to much-needed affordable housing. Among other things, *Wired*'s Adam Rogers took issue with The Ring's apparent lack of adaptability. Should the company move out, the argument goes, this giant doughnut can't easily be repurposed for new owners – and in 2021 there were reports that Apple was planning to diversify away from Silicon Valley.

Rogers also felt that the company showed insufficient care for the surrounding community and should be doing more to support local public transport infrastructure to help ease congestion on roads (most workers commuted). "The best, smartest designers and architects in the world could have tried something new," he complained. "Instead it produced a building roughly the shape of a navel, and then gazed into it."

Inevitably, an architect of Foster's stature, so publicly outspoken on his project's green credentials, a byword for innovation and ambitious new projects, and so downright prolific, will invite criticism. His track record is undeniably stellar, but not without embarrassing blemishes. Beanhill (1975), a social housing project in Milton Keynes, rapidly revealed itself to be dysfunctional, with leaking flat roofs, condensation and poor insulation, all of which required urgent correction. The multiple functions of the Sainsbury Centre's cavernous interior, from dining to teaching to public exhibitions, generated noise overspill from one area to another.

Similarly, an absence of partitioning coupled with reflective hard surfaces at the Cambridge University Faculty of Law (1995) allowed a constant stream of competing sounds to distract readers in the library. In his 2012 TED talk "Why architects need to use their ears", sound consultant Julian Treasure cited Foster's Business Academy Bexley (2003) as "designed like a corporate headquarters, with a vast central atrium and classrooms leading off it with no back walls at all. The children couldn't hear their teachers. They had to go back in and spend £600,000 putting the walls in."

Such issues highlight a flaw that journalist Rowan Moore, among others, has detected in the architect's output, summed up in a March 2002 essay for *Prospect* as "Foster's ability to be supremely skilful in some aspects of architecture, and club-footed in others." London's Bloomberg headquarters (2017) secured a Stirling Prize and has been touted as the most sustainable office in the world, using 35 per cent less energy and 73 per cent less water than a conventional office tower, and employing passive ventilation. Yet it attracted brickbats for importing thousands of tonnes of granite from India and hundreds more of bronze from Japan. It's not the first time that the "embodied energy" of Foster's buildings – their energy costs, from extraction of raw materials and manufacture to transportation and construction – has impacted on their claims to sustainability.

The architect has long maintained his commitment to environmentally conscious design. Which begs the question: why has he built so many airports? Air travel contributes around 2.5 per cent of global CO_2 emissions annually – or around one billion tonnes; were it a country, the air industry would be within the world's top ten emitters. Rowan Moore made just that point to Foster, and received a characteristically trenchant reply, the architect arguing that the aviation industry's environmental costs compared favourably, statistically speaking, with those involved in producing a hamburger (in terms of methane from the cow, and water and energy requirements). People aren't going to stop flying; therefore, the answer was to make aviation greener. "He talks of solar-powered flight and planes made of lightweight composite materials," Moore noted.

A greener air industry benefits the planet and everyone on it, but practical advances still lag way behind well-intentioned aspirations. Foster's go-to response is to stress his faith in technology – the possibilities for converting seawater to aviation fuel and decarbonizing oceans. In short, that the future will be better – a conviction that he has held fast to since childhood.

In a 2023 article in *Architects' Journal*, Barnabas Calder praises the inspirational architect Yasmeen Lari, now aged eighty-two, who abandoned

Above. Masdar City, Abu Dhabi, 2030 (estimated).

environmentally unfriendly projects for large corporations to produce low-carbon emergency shelters instead, using locally available resources and traditional techniques. Foster is internationally respected; alongside a host of honours and awards, he has been knighted and was made a peer in 1999, making him Baron Foster of Thames Bank. Given his standing, Calder asks, why isn't he using interviews to promote meaningful reforms in taxation and regulations, doing his bit to help make decarbonization a reality?

On paper, Masdar City in Abu Dhabi sounds like the definitive Foster urban scheme: energy-efficient, with a massive solar panel farm nearby, pedestrian-friendly (cars would be driverless electric vehicles), and buildings boasting the LEED approval for carbon- and cost-effective construction that has already been bestowed on a number of his projects. Raised on a podium, and benefiting from a wind tower that sucks down air and blows it around the narrow city streets,

Above. Droneport (prototype), Venice, 2016.

Masdar City is cooler than the surrounding landscape. All this at the heart of the fossil-fuel industry. Plus, with oil ultimately a limited resource, the concept makes political sense for all UAE countries. Too good to be true?

High on naysayers' list of critiques is the question of the energy costs of building such an ambitious complex in a desert without readily available resources (solar power being a notable exception). It's faced a host of unforeseen challenges too. The project was initiated in 2006, but two years later the worldwide economic meltdown derailed progress. Currently, official figures put the city's population at 6,000 (the city is projected to house 50,000), mostly workers and students, rather than long-term residents. A futuristic eco-friendly template for urban living, or a dream forever postponed? The completion date for Masdar City is currently 2030.

For all these caveats, plenty of his company's ongoing projects, although still at development stage or yet to come to fruition, demonstrate Foster's unshakeable belief in technology as a means of improving the human condition and broadening humanity's horizons. Take the prototype "droneport" that went on display at the 2016 Venice Biennale. As other innovative companies are discovering, drones offer a potential solution to the very real problem of getting medical supplies (especially blood) to inaccessible areas in Africa. Droneports could serve as landing and departure stations for drones carrying medical supplies, but also as community hubs that house health clinics and post rooms; they would be built using locally sourced materials. Rwanda hosted a pilot project. Who knows what the coming decade will bring?

Foster's enthusiasm for the possibilities of space travel and extra-terrestrial habitation goes back to his days as an *Eagle* reader, so it's inevitable that he should wish to play his part in making them happen. In 2014, Foster + Partners became involved in the European Space Agency's Lunar Habitation Project, exploring the possibilities of 3D printing four-person homes on the Moon's surface using regolith – the soil on the lunar surface. This naturally led to discussions with NASA about similar projects for Mars, though both projects remain speculative.

Then again, visionary schemes have a habit of becoming reality in Norman Foster's world. In one sketch for the Willis Faber & Dumas Headquarters, he had noted that an enveloping 3D bubble – allowing for natural ventilation, for the structure to breathe, while reducing energy demands – would be ideal for the job, but that they had neither the time nor the technical expertise to make it happen. Thirty years later, that's pretty much exactly what Foster + Partners created for the Philological Library at the Free University of Berlin (2004).

Any survey of innovative modern architecture, and its growing engagement with sustainability, must include Norman Foster. Over the past fifty years, he has repeatedly challenged, then transcended, architectural conventions to create "celebratory" spaces – a term of which he's particularly fond. He ranks among the greatest architects of our time. Eighty-eight years old in 2023, he remains disarmingly optimistic about the future. Asked in 2022 by the BBC's John Wilson about whether he'd consider retiring, he replied firmly, "Why should I? I enjoy doing what I do."

He's still building the future.
Edwin Heathcote, *Financial Times*, 2023

[01] Millau Viaduct, France, 2004. [02] Willis Building, Ipswich, 1975. [03, 04] Sainsbury Centre, Norwich, 1978. [05] Renault Centre, Swindon, 1982.

[06, 07] HSBC Headquarters, Hong Kong, 1986.

[08] Terminal at Stansted Airport, London, 1991. [09] Torre del Collserola, Barcelona, 1991. [10, 11] Carré d'Art, Nîmes, 1993.

[12, 13] Kings Norton Library, Cranfield, 1993.
[14] Lycée Albert Camus, Fréjus, 1993.

[15, 16] Metro, Bilbao, 1995. [17] Clyde Auditorium, Scotland, 1997. [18] American Air Museum at the Imperial War Museum, Duxford, 1997. [19, 20] Commerzbank Tower, Frankfurt, 1997.

離港區
Departures Zone 2

中華航空　China Airline
大韓航空　韓亞航空
瑞士航空公司
非律賓航空公司
國泰航空

[21] Hong Kong International Airport, Chek Lap Kok, 1998. [22, 23] Great Court of the British Museum, London, 1999.

[24, 25, 26] Canary Wharf Tube station, London, 1999. [27] Reichstag, Berlin, 1999.
[28] Millennium Bridge, London, 2000. [29, 30] 8 Canada Square, London, 2002.

[31, 32] The Gherkin (30 St Mary Axe), London, 2003. [33] City Hall, London, 2002.
[34, 35] Moor House, London, 2004. [36] Sage, Gateshead, 2004.

89

Norman Foster

[37] Philological Library, Berlin, 2005. [38, 39] Dresden Hauptbahnhof, Germany, 2006.
[40] Hearst Tower, New York, 2006. [41] 2006 Leslie Dan Faculty of Pharmacy, Toronto, 2006.

[42, 43] International Terminal, Beijing Capital International Airport, Beijing, 2007.
[44, 45] Wembley Stadium, London, 2007. [46, 47] Willis Building, London, 2008.

[48, 49] The Bow, Calgary 2012. [50] Citibank Headquarters, Hangzhou, 2017.
[51] Bloomberg Building, London, 2017. [52, 53] Apple Park, Cupertino, 2018.

[54]

[55]

Picture Credits

The publishers would like to thank the following sources for their kind permission to reproduce the pictures in this book.

Alamy /Aardvark 60/andrew parker 56/Arcaid Images 4–5, 26, 46, 53, 70–1, 97/architecture UK 20/BRIAN ANTHONY 100/Craig Jack Photographic 108t/David Bleeker Architectural 99/Dennis Gilbert-VIEW 58/Heritage Image Partnership Ltd 12/Ian Dagnall 55/imageBROKER.com GmbH & Co. KG 66/James Morris-VIEW 62–3/Jason Friend Photography Ltd 83/Maen Zayyad 54/mauritius images GmbH 104/Mavil/Peter Treanor 110/Petr Svarc 81/Sipa US 108b/Stockimo 38–9/Robert Evans 80/Weijie Li 96. **Bridgeman** /Bernd Tschakert 90–1. **Getty Images** /Bojan Brecelj 07/ Construction Photography/Avalon 78–9, 101/Dan Kitwood 67/FREDERIC J. BROWN 40/Geography Photos 50–1, 52b/Heritage Images 29/Jon Hicks 08/View Pictures 61. **Michael Elkin** 17t. **Norman Foster Foundation** 13, 14–5, 18, 23. **Pexels** /Mike Bird 87. **Shutterstock** /360b 68/365 Focus Photography 82/AC Manley 52t/Alastair Wallace 95/Aydin.Q 109/ BOULENGER Xavier 59/Carsten Pauly 93/Chrispictures 105/Cory Woodruff 106/Coward Lion 73/david muscroft 48–9/Felix Lipov 94/JHVEPhoto 107/ Kiev.Victor 86/Kristi Blokhin 75t/MACH Photos 75b/manfredxy 69/Marco Rubino 57/Markus Mainka 92/Matej Kastelic 76–7/Matt Biggin 87/Menno Schaefer 103/Philip Bird LRPS CPAGB 84–5/photo.ua 98/Ramon Espelt Photography 64/roberaten 72/Rosanne de Vries 65/Sven Hansche 74/ Todamo 102/Tupungato (Interior of Reichstag) 02/VOJTa Herout 35. **Tecno/ Foster + Partners** 24. **Tim Street-Porter** 17b. **Unsplash** /Ben Griffiths 30. **WikiArquitectura/The Architecture Encyclopedia** 44–5.

Every effort has been made to acknowledge correctly and contact the source/ copyright holder of the images. Welbeck Publishing Group apologizes for any unintentional errors which will be corrected in future editions of this book.

[54, 55] The Pavilion, University of Pennsylvania, Philadelphia, 2021. [56] Salesforce Tower, Sydney, 2022. **Opposite.** International Terminal, Beijing Capital International Airport, Beijing, 2007.

MIX
Paper | Supporting
responsible forestry
FSC® C144853
FSC
www.fsc.org

Published in 2024 by OH! Life

An imprint of Welbeck Non-Fiction Limited, part of Welbeck Publishing Group.
Offices in London, 20 Mortimer Street, London W1T 3JW, and Sydney, Level 17,
207 Kent Street, Sydney NSW 2000 Australia.
www.welbeckpublishing.com

Text and Design © Welbeck Non-Fiction Limited 2024

Cover image: Hearst Tower. Courtesy Shutterstock/A G Baxter

A CIP catalogue record for this book is available from the British Library.

ISBN 970 1 83861-202-3

Publisher: Lisa Dyer
Copyeditor: Katie Hewett
Design: James Pople; original concept by www.gradedesign.com
Production controller: Arlene Lestrade

Printed and bound in China

10 9 8 7 6 5 4 3 2 1